DATE			

We Were Here

We Were Here

A Short History

of Time Capsules

Patricia Seibert

The Millbrook Press   Brookfield, Connecticut

To **Paul Hudson**, cofounder of
the International Time Capsule Society,
for sharing his knowledge and enthusiasm

Library of Congress Cataloging-in-Publication Data
Seibert, Patricia.
We were here : a short history of time capsules/
by Patricia Seibert.
p. cm.
Includes index.
ISBN 0-7613-0423-1 (lib. bdg.)
1. Civilization—History—Miscellanea—Juvenile literature.
2. Time capsules—History—Juvenile literature. [1. Time
capsules. 2. Civilization—History—Miscellanea.] I. Title.
CB151 .S385 2002   00-041873

Published by The Millbrook Press, Inc.
2 Old New Milford Road
Brookfield, Connecticut 06804
www.millbrookpress.com

Cover photographs courtesy of © Erich Lessing/Art
Resource, NY: (pyramids), © Corbis/Bettmann (early
time capsule), Brown Brothers (Rosetta Stone)

Photographs courtesy of Art Resource, NY: pp. 3 (© Erich
Lessing), 9 (both © Scala); Oglethorpe University Archives:
pp. 5, 18, 22; UPI/Corbis-Bettmann: pp. 8, 11, 17, 27;
© Corbis/Bettmann: pp. 10, 14 (left), 20; Brown Brothers:
pp. 15, 23; AP/Wide World Photos: p. 14 (right); Matsushita
Electric (Panasonic): p. 28; Archive Photos: pp. 30-31
(© Reuters/William Philpott); Pentagram: p. 31 (right);
Jim Estrin/NYT Pictures: p. 33; NASA: p. 37

Contents

Chapter 1

WHAT IS A TIME CAPSULE ?

A time capsule is a container that holds a collection of items. The container, large or small, is sealed so that the items will be preserved until some time in the future.

Time capsules usually come with instructions telling when they should be opened. People select items for a time capsule with the idea that those items will convey information about the present to whoever opens the time capsule in the future.

Before the creation of the first object called a "time capsule," there were projects that had some similari-

ties to time capsules. These projects were also different in some significant ways.

More than five thousand years ago, the pyramids of Egypt were built. Inside these great stone monuments, the Egyptians placed the bodies of their dead rulers, called pharaohs. Treasures made of gold and furniture that had belonged to the pharaohs were also placed inside the pyramids. Wives and servants who died after a pharaoh died were often entombed in the pyramid along with the ruler.

The bodies were mummified, which means they were treated with special substances and wrapped round and round with many strips of cloth. Mummification helps preserve dead bodies. Scientists in modern times have studied the mummies, the gold treasures, and the other contents of the pyramids. The scientists have learned much about ancient

Artifacts and paintings found in the pyramids have provided historians with a tremendous amount of information on daily life in Egypt nearly 3,000 years ago. Although they have served the identical function, pyramids are not considered true time capsules because they were never designed to be opened at all—much less at a specific time. It is just fortunate that the Egyptians believed in an afterlife where people would actually need their day-to-day implements, thus affording us a glimpse of their lives. Shown here are a sarcophagus from about 900 B.C. (*right*), the entrance hall of the Tomb of Sennefer from the same period, and the royal throne of the famous King Tutankhamen, depicting the young pharaoh and his wife (*facing page*).

Emperor Ch'in Shih Huang Ti, who ruled China from 221-210 B.C., took his armies to his tomb. More than 8,000 life-size terra-cotta replicas of infantrymen, cavalry, archers, charioteers, and officers unearthed in 1974 quite unintentionally conveyed information to the modern world about ancient Chinese war practices.

Egypt because they could study what was saved inside the pyramids.

Over two thousand years ago in China, emperors were buried in large underground chambers. The chambers were filled with objects that the ancient Chinese thought were beautiful and precious—objects like ceramic vases and jewelry. Life-size pottery statues of soldiers and horses were made especially to put into the burial chambers.

For hundreds of years people have stored away special items in the foundations of important buildings. A foundation block would be hollowed out so the collection of items could be put inside. Often, people used the cornerstone, a foundation block at the corner of a building, as a place to put a box filled with important papers, coins, and other objects.

The idea was that one day, many years in the future, the building would fall down or be torn down. Then the hidden items would be revealed and show people of the future a little bit about how things were in the past.

The Egyptian pyramids and Chinese burial chambers held collections of items, just as time capsules do, but the collections were not planned as a way to

The next step along the road to true time capsules was the cornerstone. Materials were deliberately placed in the corners of new buildings, often with great fanfare, as messages for the future. The problem was, the building had to fall down or be destroyed before the messages could be delivered—thus cornerstones, like the earlier burial chambers, are not true time capsules, though they serve the same function. Former New York governor Alfred E. Smith is shown here laying the cornerstone of the Empire State Building. Did he inscribe something in the cement or place some objects under stone as was the custom of the time? We will find out only if someone takes a wrecking ball to one of New York City's most famous structures.

share information with people living in the future. These collections were stored in the pyramids and burial chambers for other purposes. The ancient peoples were following their religious beliefs. They were also acting out of respect for their dead rulers.

The collections in the building cornerstones were planned with the hope that people in the future would find them and learn from them—but not on a specified date. Cornerstones differ from time capsules because a time capsule is made with the idea that someone in the future will examine its contents on a certain date.

Of course, making sure that people many years in the future will know when to open the time capsule—and just where it is located—can be very tricky. It is easy to lose track of a time capsule.

Chapter 2

WHO INVENTED TIME CAPSULES ?

It is not entirely clear who was the first to create what could be considered an actual time capsule. It is easier to pinpoint when the name "time capsule" was first used. The term was first used in connection with a project for the 1939 New York World's Fair.

A big company named Westinghouse wanted to produce a special project to display at the fair. At first the project was referred to as a "time bomb." Bombs are designed to deliver explosions and destruction to a specific target. The idea for the World's Fair project was to deliver a "slice of time" to people living five thousand years in the future.

TIME CAPSULE

Top, with device for hoisting

Mark where future Archaeologists will saw to open

Outer shell of Cupaloy, a copper alloy hard as steel

Pyrex glass inner envelope

7 FEET 6 INCHES

Also, the long narrow container that was used for the project looked like a bomb. The container was filled with all kinds of odds and ends that people used in their daily lives. An alarm clock, a safety pin, and a lady's hat were three of the items put into the container.

Here is a selection of objects chosen to be included in the Westinghouse time capsule. Although many of the objects have a dated look more than sixty years later, we still can figure out what they all are—but will people thousands of years from now recognize a cog wheel, or eyeglasses, or corrugated board?

But the name "bomb" did not seem quite right for a project that was supposed to make people feel excited and happy. After a little while, the container began to be referred to as a "time capsule." The term caught the public's imagination, and a new term was coined for the English language.

Even though the name "time capsule" was first used for the World's Fair project, other people had created projects that also could be defined as time capsules. In fact, just a few years before the World's Fair, a big project was started that is sometimes called the granddaddy of all time capsules.

Westinghouse engineers were well aware of the care needed to preserve documents for 5,000 years. They made their capsule waterproof, shockproof, and easy to pull from the ground, and they even scored a section to make it easier for future archaeologists to saw it open. They look proud and confident, but were they successful? We'll know in about 4,940 years.

Chapter 3

A COLOSSAL TIME CAPSULE: THE CRYPT OF CIVILIZATION

——◆——

At Oglethorpe University in Atlanta, Georgia, Dr. Thornwell Jacobs was making plans for what he called the "Crypt of Civilization." Dr. Jacobs published an article describing his plan in the November 1936 issue of a magazine called *Scientific American*.

Dr. Jacobs was the president of Oglethorpe University. Many buildings on the Oglethorpe campus were constructed of granite and were built on a foundation of Appalachian bedrock. The location Jacobs chose for his giant time capsule was a large, basement-level room in one of the granite buildings—Hearst Hall. The word "crypt" means underground room.

The room in Hearst Hall had been the location of a swimming pool. Its dimensions were 10 by 20 feet (3 by 6 meters), and it was 10 feet (3 meters) high. The stone roof above the large chamber was 7 feet (2 meters) thick, and the stone floor below it was 2 feet (60 cm) thick.

To create the time capsule, the chamber floor was raised with concrete. Damp-proofing material was applied. The walls were lined with porcelain enamel.

Once the Crypt was filled with its many items, it was to be sealed up. (The actual sealing of the Crypt took place in 1940.) A specially made stainless steel door, 9½ feet (almost 3 meters) tall and a little over 4 feet (1 meter) wide, would be welded into place. The door would be the only thing visible once the Crypt was closed.

When Dr. Jacobs came up with the idea for his project, he had been studying ancient history. He knew how hard it was to uncover information about human

Dr. Thornwell Jacobs was an educator, clergyman, and author. In the course of his teaching at Oglethorpe University, he became concerned about the dearth of information on ancient civilizations–a problem that eventually led him to formulate a plan for preserving a record of contemporary society for posterity.

CRYPT OF CIVILIZATION

IN CONSIDERATION OF GIFTS MADE BY

A. FRIEND

TO THE "CRYPT OF CIVILIZATION" IN THE YEAR A. D. 1939, ANY DECENDENDANT OF THE ABOVE NAMED CONTRIBUTOR, OF THE 187TH GENERATION, UPON PRESENTATION OF THIS CARD, WILL BE ADMITTED TO THE OPENING OF THE CRYPT ON THURSDAY, MAY 28TH, A. D. 8113, NOON.

OGLETHORPE UNIVERSITY

OGLETHORPE 1940 TO 8113 UNIVERSITY

A copy of the above card in imperishable metal may be had by addressing the Archivist, Oglethorpe University, Ga., Price—$1.00.

Extra copies of this bulletin may be had at five cents each.

One of Dr. Jacobs's more charming, if not terribly practical, ideas for having people remember the existence of his time capsule was to issue the ultimate in engraved invitations. Donors of $1.00 to the project received the above invitation engraved in "imperishable metal." It's always nice to have sufficient advance notice before an important event!

beings who had lived thousands of years before. Yet he saw that some kinds of information endured for many, many centuries. He studied very old objects and writings in ancient languages that helped him learn about people from long ago.

Dr. Jacobs studied mainly recorded human history. This period of history began when human beings started organizing their lives and keeping records about their lives in ways that people today can relate to.

Many historians in the 1930s agreed on the starting point for recorded human history. They said it began a little over six thousand years in the past—actually 6,177 years before 1936, the year Jacobs started planning his time capsule project. Dr. Jacobs decided to add 6,177 years to 1936, and he came up with the year 8113 as the time for the grand opening ceremony of the Crypt of Civilization.

After more than sixty centuries, how would anyone ever know about the existence of the Crypt? Dr. Jacobs planned to have instructions placed in many libraries and archives all over the world. The instructions would explain where the Crypt was and when to open it. He hoped that, as new libraries were created, the instructions would be passed on to them.

What kinds of things did Dr. Jacobs put into the Crypt? He included things that were as ordinary as a plastic Donald Duck toy. He also wanted to include as much of the knowledge collected in encyclopedias and books as he could.

All those books would take up a great deal of room, even in a time capsule as huge as the Crypt. So the pages of each book were photographed with microfilm cameras. More than six hundred thousand pages were photographed—one page at a time.

The microfilm images are 1 by 1½ inches (2.5 by 4 cm). The images will need to be magnified many times before the words on them can be read. Even though the microfilm was going to be stored inside the Crypt, it first was sealed inside stainless steel containers with glass linings.

There were also unusual things, like a machine to teach the English language, in case those who opened the Crypt did not know how to speak or read English. The machine, specially invented for the Crypt, was called the Language Integrator.

The Language Integrator has a crank to turn by hand. When the crank is turned, a metal page flips up.

Dr. Jacobs is shown with T. K. Peters, then Director of Archives at Oglethorpe University, examining one of the steel vaults that will protect items in the Crypt. In the foreground are two dolls dressed in the style of the late 1930s. Among other items chosen for inclusion in the Crypt were chewing gum, popular soft drinks, Toscanini records, newspapers, and recordings of speeches by prominent persons. Toys included a Donald Duck, the Lone Ranger, and Lincoln Logs. The contents of a typical lady's purse were included, as were 1940 models of a Royal typewriter, a National cash register, and a White sewing machine.

A picture of an object is engraved on the metal page. The name of the object is engraved on the page, too. The hand-cranking action also causes a phonograph record to be played so, at the same time the picture is displayed, the record plays the name of the object that is pictured.

Some people have said that this machine to help people of the future understand and interpret the English language is like a mechanical version of the famous Rosetta Stone. The Rosetta Stone was an actual slab of black stone inscribed about 200 B.C. A decree about a king who ruled Egypt at the time had been carved into the stone three times using three different systems of writing.

The process of photographing books and placing them on microfilm seems primitive today when tens of thousands of pages can easily be condensed into computer zip files. But in Jacobs's day the concept of storing more than 640,000 pages of text in microfilm format was an innovative one. In fact, Jacobs's curator, T. K. Peters, had been the inventor of the microfilm camera, using 35-mm film to photograph documents.

The decree was written once in ancient Greek. It was written twice in ancient Egyptian using two different forms of writing. One form of writing was called hieroglyphics, and the other was called demotic script. When the Rosetta Stone was discovered a little over two hundred years ago, only the Greek section could be read and understood by scholars. By studying the Rosetta Stone, scholars and scientists were able to figure out that the two Egyptian sections said the same thing as the Greek section.

The Rosetta Stone was the key to helping scholars and scientists in the 1800s learn how to interpret two written languages that had been used thousands of years earlier. This knowledge made it possible to interpret other exam-

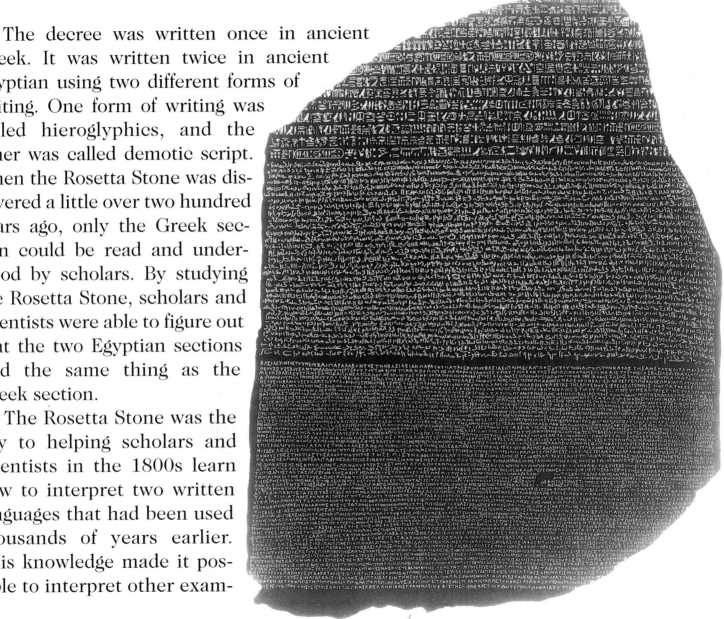

ples of the two ancient Egyptian languages that had been found in other places.

For instance, some paintings and carvings inside the great pyramids of Egypt included hieroglyphics, which is a form of writing that uses pictures or symbols. The pictures or symbols sometimes have a meaning and sometimes are used to stand for sounds. Sometimes, the pictures or symbols are used to represent both meanings and sounds. The discovery of the Rosetta Stone helped researchers interpret the hieroglyphics uncovered in the pyramids.

If a time capsule is to be sealed for thousands of years, it may be necessary for those who open the capsule to have a way to interpret the language on documents contained in the capsule. It is almost impossible to imagine the changes that will take place over the next six thousand years. Yet people have studied and learned about how people on Earth lived six thousand years ago. Maybe it will be possible for someone on Earth in the far-distant future to try to understand us and our activities. And just maybe the Crypt of Civilization will be a source of important historical information for the citizens living in 8113. Dr. Jacobs truly hoped so.

Chapter 4

TIME CAPSULES
ALL OVER THE WORLD

———◆———

In 1990, the fiftieth anniversary of the Crypt of Civilization was celebrated at Oglethorpe University. In that same year, the International Time Capsule Society (ITCS) was founded at Oglethorpe. One of the main purposes of the ITCS is to register time capsules. Any organization or person who creates a time capsule can send information about its location to the ITCS. There are now thousands of time capsules all over the world. No one has saved records about the location of most of them.

Many different groups and individuals create time capsules for many different reasons. Often a group of

When the town of Hawthorne, New York, built its schoolhouse in 1910, town officials placed something in the cornerstone. When the building was eventually sold and scheduled to be demolished in 1975, it was billed as an exciting event—a link from the community's past to its future. But, alas, as seen by the disappointed expressions on the faces of onlookers, the link turned out to be just a roll of rotted newspaper. Modern preservation techniques hopefully will prevent such future disappointments.

school students creates a time capsule at the beginning of the school year with plans to open it at the end of the year. Or the students will plan to open it five years after they graduate from high school. These are important and worthwhile projects even if they do not require the same kind of planning as a time capsule that is supposed to preserve its contents for a century or more.

Time capsules that are supposed to be opened in fifty or one hundred years or more are often planned as part of celebrations by cities, large organizations, or corporations. These time-capsule projects are sometimes very elaborate.

A time capsule is "millennial" if it is scheduled to be opened in one thousand years or more. Most time-capsule projects are not millennial. When the calendar year changed to 2000, more millennial time capsules than usual were created to celebrate the occasion.

Before the creation of all the time capsules to mark the year 2000, one of the best-known millennial time capsule projects had been created in 1970 in Japan as part of the celebration for the world's fair called Expo '70. Two identical time capsules, which were in the shape of spheres and had identical contents, were buried on the grounds of Osaka Castle.

When it was created for Japan's World Exposition Time Capsule, Expo '70 was considered very modern and high-tech, billing itself as the most comprehensive time capsule of the twentieth century. But for its first scheduled opening in 2000, it did not appear to be high-tech at all. The Osaka capsule did not contain a personal computer, a cell phone, or even a compact disc player—because none of those items had been invented by 1970. If the contents of the capsule seem outdated to us in just thirty years, what will they be in another hundred years? Will people even know what the items were or what they were for in a thousand years?

The one buried the deepest is scheduled to be opened in five thousand years, which will be 6970. The second capsule is buried at a shallower depth, and it is scheduled to be opened many times—the first time in the year 2000. After that, it is to be opened every one hundred years, so that the contents can be checked to see how well they are being preserved.

The continual opening of the second capsule will also help remind people about the first capsule. That helps increase the chances that, if human life on Earth continues in some form, the first capsule can still be located five thousand years from now.

At the beginning of the year 2000, turn-of-the-century celebrations all over the world included time capsules. U.S. President Bill Clinton participated in a celebration that included a time capsule for America. America's time capsule, the National Millennium Time Capsule, is scheduled to be opened in 2100. It will not be buried. Instead, it will be stored for one hundred years in the National Archives. Americans from famous authors to schoolchildren made suggestions about what to include. Inside the time capsule there is, among many other items, a Hostess Twinkie.

U.S. President Bill Clinton and First Lady Hillary Rodham Clinton open a prototype of the National Millennium Time Capsule on December 31, 1999. The capsule, designed in the graphic form of an American flag, is constructed of materials chosen to withstand time and to symbolize America's past, present, and future. Stainless steel represents the industrial past, silicon bronze symbolizes the communications era of the present, and titanium represents the future.

The Times Capsule, a project of the newspaper *The New York Times*, is a millennial time capsule. The year 3000 is the target date for opening this capsule. The newspaper held a competition to see who would design the best time-capsule container. Designers, architects, and engineers from all over the world submitted their ideas.

A Spanish architect, Santiago Calatrava, was the winner. He said his design looked something like a flower. It turned out to be a very expensive, and a very heavy, flower. *The New York Times* paid $60,000 to have the capsule made out of stainless steel. The capsule weighs two tons and is on permanent display at the American Museum of Natural History in New York City.

People from many countries contributed ideas about what objects to include in the Times Capsule. Of course, copies of *The New York Times* are included. The copies are not on regular newsprint, though. Some copies are on acid-free archival paper. There are also copies that are "microengraved" on a disk that is 2 inches (5 cm) wide. The disk can be read by using a very high-powered microscope.

The ability to do microsize engraving on a special 2-inch disk was a new technological process when the

The flowing shape of *The New York Times* millennial capsule (*opposite*) seems totally futuristic—today, at least.

Times Capsule was created. Many thousands of pages could be placed on the 2-inch disk. Compare the microfilm technology used just sixty years earlier in the Crypt of Civilization. Each microfilm image measured 1 inch by 1½ inches (2.5 by 4 cm), but held only one page of a book or newspaper.

Chapter 5

A FEW OTHER INTERESTING TIME CAPSULES

CENTURY SAFE

This project was started long before the term "time capsule" was coined. It was created in 1876 to celebrate the one-hundredth anniversary of the United States.

A woman named Mrs. Charles Diehm, a New York publisher, wanted to celebrate the centennial of the United States by putting a collection of important items into a safe that would be opened in one hundred years to help celebrate the two-hundredth anniversary (bicentennial) of the United States.

Many autographs and photographs of Civil War officers and government officials were included in the safe. The opening of the safe did take place in 1976 as planned. The ceremony was attended by the president of the United States, Gerald Ford. Since the Century Safe was created so long ago with the idea of opening it at a certain time in the future, some time-capsule experts say the safe may be the first *real* time capsule.

VISIONS OF MARS

All the information in this time capsule is collected on a CD-ROM. The Visions of Mars compact disc was a collection of artists' ideas about Mars. Books, paintings, and audio files were included. Copies of the CD-ROM went on sale to the public. Any money raised was to help pay for further exploration of Mars.

The compact disc was supposed to be carried to Mars by a Russian spacecraft in 1996, but the spacecraft failed shortly after take-off.

The director of the Visions of Mars project said that the CD-ROM was, "in a way, the first time capsule sent to another planet." (Since there was no way to specify the target date for retrieving and playing the CD-ROM, some would say it was not exactly a time capsule.)

The people who worked on the project hoped that human space travelers would land on Mars in fifty or one hundred years and be able to locate the CD-ROM.

Will future astronauts actu- ally landing on Mars recognize the romanticized drawings of the planet that are sent up from Earth today?

Instructions for playing the CD-ROM with a laser were included with the spacecraft. The instructions were written in five languages.

MIT SLOAN DIGITAL TIME CAPSULE

The information in this time capsule is saved electronically on computers. Instead of burying the time capsule, the people working on this project encrypted it—scrambling all the electronic information, or data, so that the information cannot be read unless a secret code is used.

This project was created in 1999. What was saved on the computers? Information on all kinds of topics that had appeared on the Internet on Web pages was included. Copies of the Web pages were "captured" on the Digital Time Capsule computers.

At the beginning of the twenty-first century, developments on the Internet, like how Web pages are designed and used, are happening very fast. Because of the fast pace of the changes, this all-digital time capsule will be unlocked only five years after it was created. Even after such a short time, people involved with the project expect that what is saved on the computers will seem out of date.

Chapter 6

THE IMPACT OF TIME CAPSULES

***

Since the term "time capsule" was coined in the middle of the twentieth century, the term has become extremely popular—even more popular than time capsules themselves. People use the term to describe many things—a collection of objects, a list of facts, or even a sunken ship—in fact, almost anything that represents a particular time in a particular place.

Newspapers and magazines often publish articles that are referred to as time capsules. These articles often list events or objects from an earlier time. When people make actual time capsules, they usually select objects from the time they are living in.

Many scientists point out that it is foolish to think that a collection of items, especially a collection that people select themselves, can give an accurate picture of life at a certain time. In fact, some scientists say that landfills are actually the best time capsules. The contents of a garbage dump can reveal what is used by a society and how much is used. Experts say that many of the plastic items that people throw away will last for many thousands of years, even tens of thousands of years.

Perhaps the greatest value of the time capsules that people make is the thinking that is required to select what should be included in the capsules. No matter what is learned by those who open a time capsule—or even if no one ever finds it and opens it—the people who create a time capsule learn many things about themselves.

MAKING A Time Capsule

There are all types of time capsules. If you make a time capsule, here are some things to think about:

1. KEEP GOOD RECORDS.

Make sure that someone in the future will know when to open the capsule. Are the instructions clear about the location of the time capsule?

2. CHOOSE THE RIGHT KIND OF CONTAINER.

Almost anything—a box, a tube, a jar—will do if you plan to store the capsule for a year or two on a closet shelf. If you want to bury your capsule, you will need a special container that keeps out water. In fact, you will need to research which kinds of containers can preserve items in the best way.

3. COLLECT MEANINGFUL ITEMS TO PUT INSIDE.

When will the time capsule be opened? By whom? Your plan for your time capsule will help you make choices about what to include.

One time capsule expert says: Simple is best. He suggests including a statement about yourself written with a No. 2 pencil. Pencil writing lasts much better than writing from an ink pen because ink changes more over time. (Materials that change just a little over time are referred to as "stable." Materials that change a lot are called "unstable." Stable materials are better for time capsules that will not be opened for years and years.)

If you plan a simple time capsule, have fun! If you want a time capsule that will preserve its contents for a long time, do research at the library and on the Internet. (The Smithsonian Institution has some time capsule information on its Web site.) Your research and planning will help you have good results with your time capsule.

Web Sites

RELATED TO TIME CAPSULES

These Web sites are current up to the last moment before publication.

http://www.oglethorpe.edu/itcs/

This is the site of the International Time Capsule Society. The society is located at Oglethorpe University in Atlanta, Georgia.

The Web site offers eight tips on how to organize a time capsule as well as a worldwide time-capsule registry. More information about the Crypt of Civilization and pictures of the Crypt can be found here, too.

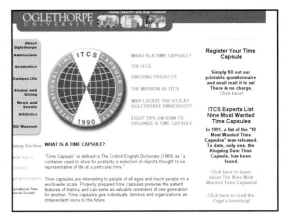

http://vraptor.jpl.nasa.gov/voyager/record.html

The National Aeronautics and Space Administration (NASA) has information on this Web page about a special gold-plated phonograph record that carries a message about life on Earth. NASA refers to this phonograph record as a kind of time capsule. The record was sent out into space on both *Voyager 1* and *Voyager 2*, which were launched in 1977.

THE *NEW YORK TIMES* CAPSULE IS INSTALLED IN CEREMONY AT AMERICAN MUSEUM OF NATURAL HISTORY'S WESTON PAVILION

Capsule On Permanent Display at Museum; Not to be Opened for 1,000 Years

New York...April 26, 2001
Ellen V. Futter, President of the American Museum of Natural History, today presided over the installation of The *New York Times* Capsule, commissioned by The *New York Times* to chronicle life in the late 20th century. The Capsule, a 5' x 5' x 5' sculpture of welded stainless steel, was designed by renowned Spanish architect Santiago Calatrava, whose entry was chosen from among 50 proposals. The Capsule was the centerpiece of the Museum's 1999 exhibition Capturing Time: The *New York Times* Capsule. In attendance at the installation were: Henry Stern, Commissioner, Department of Parks and Recreation; Jennifer Raab, Commissioner, Landmarks Preservation Commission; Jean Parker Phifer, President, Art Commission; Daniel J. Boorstin, Librarian of Congress *Emeritus* and the First Capsule Keeper; and Calatrava.

http://www.amnh.org/programs/specials/timecapsule/index.html

This is the Web address for the American Museum of Natural History in New York City. The Times Capsule created by *The New York Times* will be on permanent display in this museum, and can be accessed directly at this address.

http://www.si.edu/scmre/timecaps.html

The Smithsonian Institution has a special department called the Conservational Analytical Laboratory (CAL). One of its purposes is to distribute scientific information about how to preserve museum collections and related materials.

The Laboratory has several online brochures to give information about questions that people often ask. One of the online brochures is all about time capsules. This Web address is for the time capsule brochure that is online. There are suggestions about how to make a time capsule, where to buy one, what to put in it, and conditions that can help preserve it.

http://parallel.park.org/Japan/Panasonic/
time_capsule/index.html

This is an exciting Web site with lots of information about the millennial time capsule buried in Osaka, Japan, for Expo '70. There are many photos and drawings.

http://www.keo.org

This is the official Web site for KEO, an unusual time-capsule project conceived by an artist in France. The time capsule, launched into space on a satellite in 2001, will stay in orbit for 50,000 years. Then it will come back down to Earth. Many organizations, including the European Space Agency and the United Nations Educational, Scientific and Cultural Organization, have endorsed the KEO project. Up to the time of launch, anyone can contribute a message—by

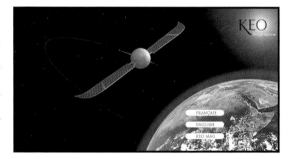

E-mail or regular mail—to be included in the time capsule. The messages will be collected on a specially designed CD-ROM. The Web site has information about how to contribute and what items besides the CD-ROM will be put in the time capsule. The Web site has lots of other information, too, including a list of answers to frequently asked questions (FAQ).

http://www.messagestothefuture.org

This Internet yearbook project has also been called a time capsule in cyberspace. The Web site describes how the project works. American students in the class of 2000 helped create a permanent record on the Internet about life as high school seniors during their graduation year.

Glossary

centennial time capsule—a time capsule that is scheduled to be opened one hundred years after its creation

commemorative time capsule—a time capsule made to honor a specific event

encyclopedic time capsule—a time capsule that includes a broad range of items representing many fields of knowledge, just as an encyclopedia covers a broad range of knowledge

inventory—the actual physical objects contained in a time capsule or the written list of those objects

millennial time capsule—a time capsule that is scheduled to be opened one thousand years after its creation

retrieval date—the date when a time capsule is scheduled to be opened

Index

Page numbers in *italics* refer to illustrations.